HOW TO DRAW™
STILL LIFE

Mark Bergin

BOOK HOUSE

S A L A R I Y A

Published in Great Britain in MMXIII by
Book House, an imprint of
The Salariya Book Company Ltd
25 Marlborough Place, Brighton BN1 1UB

3 5 7 9 8 6 4 2

Author: **Mark Bergin** was born in Hastings in 1961.
He studied at Eastbourne College of Art and has
specialised in historical reconstructions as well as
aviation and maritime subjects since 1983. He lives in
Bexhill-on-Sea with his wife and three children.

Editor: Rob Walker

PB ISBN: 978-1-908973-46-7

A CIP catalogue record for this
book is available from the
British Library.

Printed and bound in China.
Printed on paper from sustainable sources.
Reprinted in MMXIII.

**WARNING: Fixatives should be
used only under adult supervision.**

Visit our websites to read
interactive **free** web books, stay up
to date with new releases, catch
up with us on the
Book House Blog, view our
electronic catalogue and more!

www.salariya.com
Free electronic versions of four of
our *You Wouldn't Want to Be* titles

www.book-house.co.uk
Online catalogue
Information books
and graphic novels

www.scribobooks.com
Fiction books

www.scribblersbooks.com
Books for babies, toddlers and
pre-school children

**www.flickr.com/photos/
salariyabookhouse**
View our photostream with sneak
previews of forthcoming titles

Join the conversation on Facebook
and Twitter by visiting
www.salariya.com

Visit
www.salariya.com
for our online catalogue and
free interactive web books.

PAPER FROM
**SUSTAINABLE
FORESTS**

Contents

Making a start

Astill life is a work of art which shows a group of objects. Almost anything works as a still-life subject. You can use natural or manmade objects, and you can arrange them artfully or draw them just as you find them.

The objects in each of these drawings have been grouped by the artist to make an interesting arrangement. Fruit, flowers and glasses have been popular with still-life artists for hundreds of years.

This book will try to give you a basic understanding of drawing and sketching your everyday surroundings. The only way to get better is to keep practising and know your subject. Start sketching and experimenting with basic objects and shapes to see how they relate to each other as a group.

Practise sketching everyday groups of objects lying around your home.

Here is an example of a 'found' subject: the shoes and keys were not deliberately arranged by the artist, but drawn just as they were.

Sketching everyday surroundings will help you understand the perspective all around you.

Drawing materials

There are many different ways to approach a drawing. Try different materials like pencils, pen and ink, brush pens, felt-tip pens and coloured pencils. Each creates quite a different result that will add variety to your drawings.

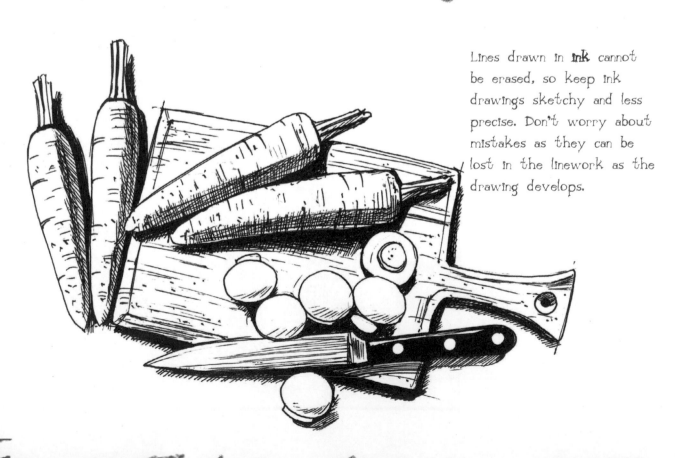

Lines drawn in **ink** cannot be erased, so keep ink drawings sketchy and less precise. Don't worry about mistakes as they can be lost in the linework as the drawing develops.

It can be tricky adding light and shade with an ink pen. Analyse your drawing. The lightest areas should be left untouched. Then apply solid areas of ink to the darkest parts. The midtones are achieved by hatching (single parallel lines) or cross—hatching (criss—crossed lines).

Felt—tips come in a range of line widths. The broader tips are good for filling in large areas of flat tone.

Hard pencils are more grey and soft pencils are blacker. Hard pencils are graded from 6H (the hardest) through 5H, 4H, 3H, 2H and H.

Soft pencils are graded from B, 2B, 3B, 4B and 5B and up to 6B (the softest).

Ways of looking

There are different ways to approach a still-life composition, from realistic drawing to abstract forms.

Try varying the amount of detail in your drawing. The more detailed, the more realistic the result. The more sketchy, the more impressionistic your composition will be.

Drawing just the outline shapes of objects can
create a more abstract composition. Look carefully
at the spaces between objects — artists call this
'negative space'.

Working in line with
some solid blocks of
shading rather than a
tonal approach can
make your drawing
very striking.

9

Perspective

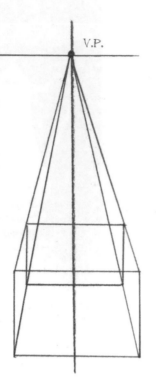

I f you look at any object from different viewpoints, you will see that the part that is closest to you looks larger, and the part furthest away from you looks smaller. Drawing in perspective is a way of creating a feeling of space — of showing three dimensions on a flat surface.

The vanishing point (V.P.) is the place in a perspective drawing where parallel lines appear to meet. The position of the vanishing point depends on the viewer's eye level. Sometimes a low viewpoint can give your drawing added drama.

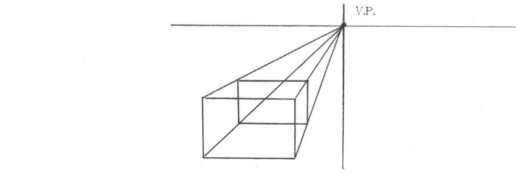

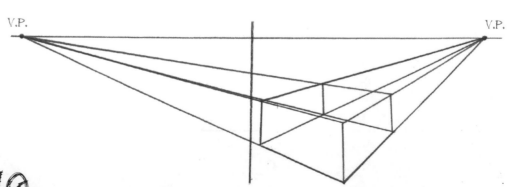

V.P. = vanishing point

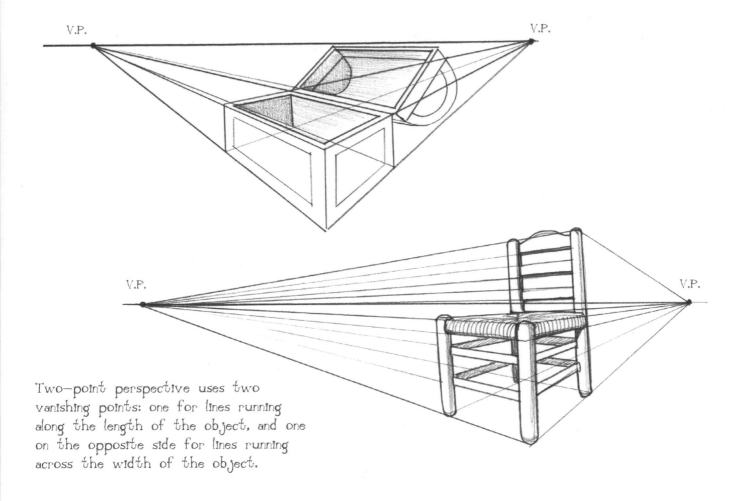

V.P.   V.P.

V.P.   V.P.

Two-point perspective uses two vanishing points: one for lines running along the length of the object, and one on the opposite side for lines running across the width of the object.

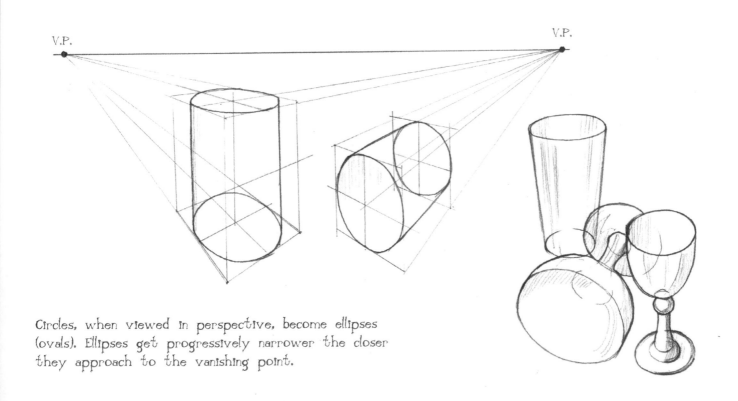

V.P.   V.P.

Circles, when viewed in perspective, become ellipses (ovals). Ellipses get progressively narrower the closer they approach to the vanishing point.

11

Using grids

Using grids will help you to draw accurately. Your viewpoint must be consistent, so keep your head in the same position once you start to draw.

Draw a squared—off grid on a piece of card and place it behind your still—life object.

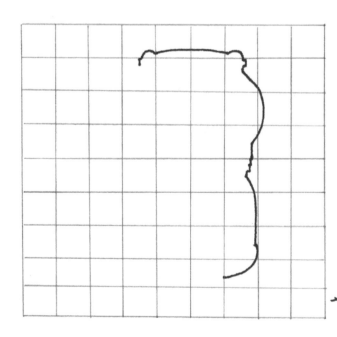

Draw a faint grid of the same proportions on your drawing paper. Then, as you look at your still—life object, you can use the two grids to gauge the exact form of the object.

Here you can see the outline being drawn in.

Draw in each section of the object, always comparing the grid against the original.

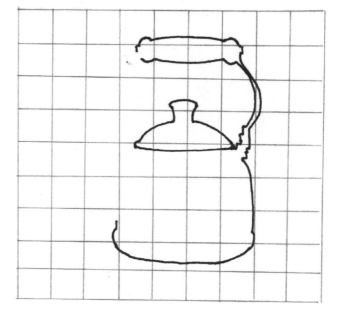

Complete the outline of your drawing using this technique to capture the correct proportions and form of the object.

Once the shape of the outline is complete, add more details to the drawing. Always refer back to the original grid for accuracy.

13

Defining form

The way light hits an object helps define its form. Using light and shade can make an object appear three—dimensional.

These examples give a simple circle the appearance of a sphere by defining the direction of the light source and then adding shading.

Light source

In this view the light comes from the side and the sphere casts an elliptical shadow.

Light source

In this view the light comes from behind and the sphere casts an almost circular shadow. The areas of shading on the sphere are furthest from the light source, facing the viewer.

Light source

In this view the light comes from above the sphere and casts an elliptical shadow. Note how this light source creates a much lower area of shading on the sphere.

Here are some samples of light sources helping to define the shape of different objects.

Light source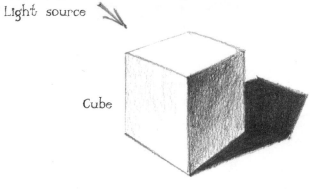

Cube

Light source

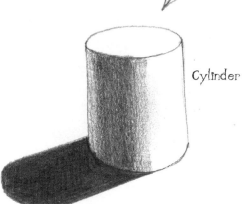

Cylinder

Light source

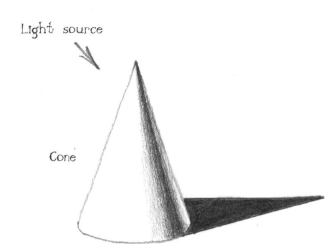

Cone

These shading techniques can then be used to define the shapes in your still life. Using different levels of shade will affect the overall tone of your drawing.

15

Inspiration

Famous artists such as Picasso, Van Gogh, Cézanne and Patrick Caulfield are great sources of inspiration for anyone interested in still life. Their styles are vastly different and give some indication of the many possible ways to approach a simple still—life subject.

Look at other artists' work when you get stuck with a particular drawing or painting problem. See how they have overcome similar problems.

16

Golden rectangles

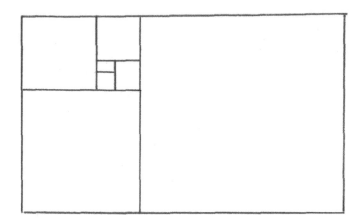

Ever since the ancient Greeks, artists have been fascinated by this graceful proportion.

1. Draw a square.

If you remove a square from your golden rectangle, the part left over is also a golden rectangle. You can keep on doing this as many times as you like.

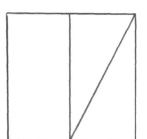

2. Divide it in half. In one half, draw a diagonal.

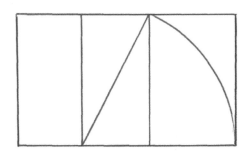

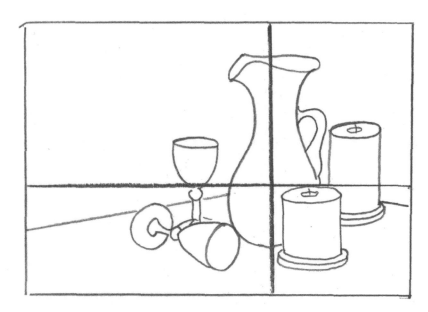

3. Setting your compasses on the ends of the diagonal, draw a curve as shown. This gives the length of your golden recatangle.

The composition of this still—life drawing is based on the golden rectangle. Note how the jug aligns with the edge of the original square.

Choosing themes

The choice of theme is wide open and individual. It can range from traditional flowers, ornaments and garden objects to a still life based purely on a single colour theme. Choose whatever inspires you.

Think of a theme you would like to draw and collect the objects you need.

Arrange your still—life objects so they create an interesting composition. These different—sized garden objects are arranged to complement each other.

18

Once you have arranged your objects, think about creating an atmosphere to suit your drawing. Here, the candlelight creates atmospheric dark shadows which greatly enhance the theme. This picture is a *memento mori*, one of the earliest forms of still life.

This still life is beach-themed. It incorporates many different objects to evoke the sense of a day at the beach.

Light and shade

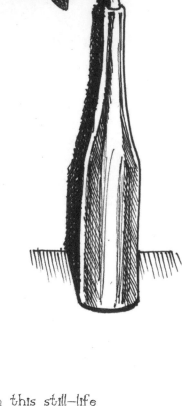

Light and shade play a major role in the outcome of your drawing. It is well worth considering the direction and strength of your light source. Both aspects add an important dimension to still-life drawing.

This drawing is front-lit with a strong light source. The object itself has little shading but it casts a strong shadow on the wall behind it.

In this still-life arrangement, the soft lighting comes from the right-hand side. Therefore the shading is mostly on the left side of the objects. Because they are brightly lit, the shading is quite muted. Cross-hatching is a good shading technique.

20

The light source
in this still life
comes from quite
a low angle and
casts dark
shadows. The
objects are
heavily shaded
because of the
low lighting.

Artificial light can create
interesting light and shade
effects. The light source in this
still life comes from the lamp at
the centre of the composition.
The light hits all the objects
at different angles, so shadows
are cast in different directions.
The lampshade also glows because
the light source is inside it.

Composition

Try framing your drawing
with a square or a
rectangle – this can make
it look completely different.

Negative space

raining yourself to really look at and perceive objects is a vital skill in still-life drawing. A good exercise to try is drawing an object by looking at the negative space only.

Start by arranging the objects for your still life as you would normally.

Negative space is the space around or between objects. By careful observation of the negative space in your still life, you will define the objects in it.

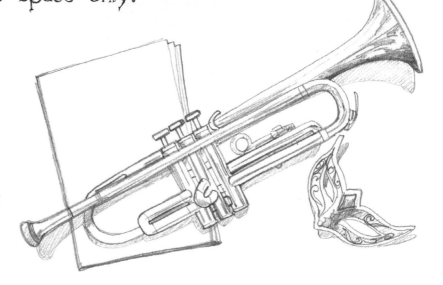

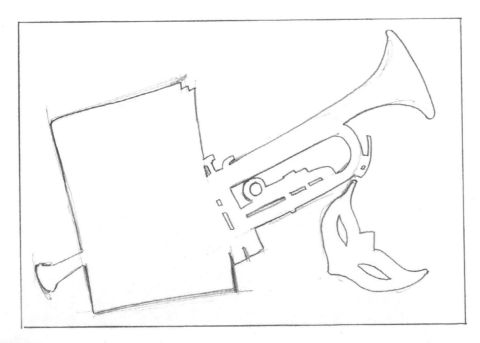

Look for the edges of each object and draw them in. This creates an outline for your negative-space drawing.

Now begin to add dark shading around the edges of the negative space. You can include the shadow of the object in a lighter tone to create more interesting compositions (as shown here).

Complete your negative-space drawing by heavily shading in all remaining areas. The results can give an abstract look to your drawing.

If an object has a very distinctive shape it may need very little visual information to describe it.

Even in an ordinary drawing, observation of the negative space is a very good way to spot any faults or mistakes.

23

Household objects

This section guides you through the process of drawing objects from basic shapes to completion.

Organise your still life objects into the best composition.

Draw a 'wire-frame' outline of each of the objects. Starting with the oval bases will help you to position them correctly.

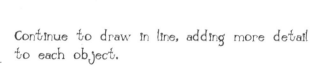

Continue to draw in line, adding more detail to each object.

Try not to draw these construction lines too heavily, as you may wish to erase some of them later.

Proportions

Hold your pencil at arm's length and use it to judge the proportions of the objects in your still life.

24

Drawing in the background drapery.

Consider the direction and strength of your light source. In this still life the light source is quite strong and comes from the right—hand side.

Add shading to the side furthest from the light source. The darkest areas of tone will be where no light reaches.

Add all remaining details and shading to give each object a lifelike appearance.

Use an eraser to lift out white highlights where light reflects on shiny surfaces.

Remove any unwanted construction lines.

25

Chair and jacket

I mpressive still—life compositions can be made from the most ordinary everyday objects.

Start by drawing a box in perspective.

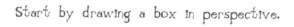

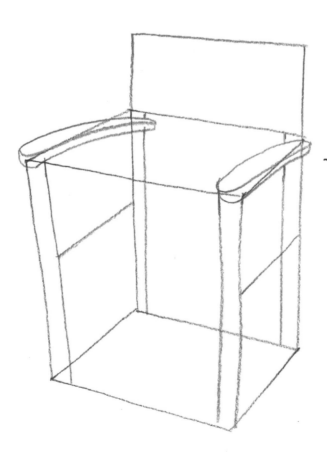

Construct the main section of the chair within the box area. Now draw in the back of the chair above it.

Remember to draw these construction lines lightly so they can easily be erased later.

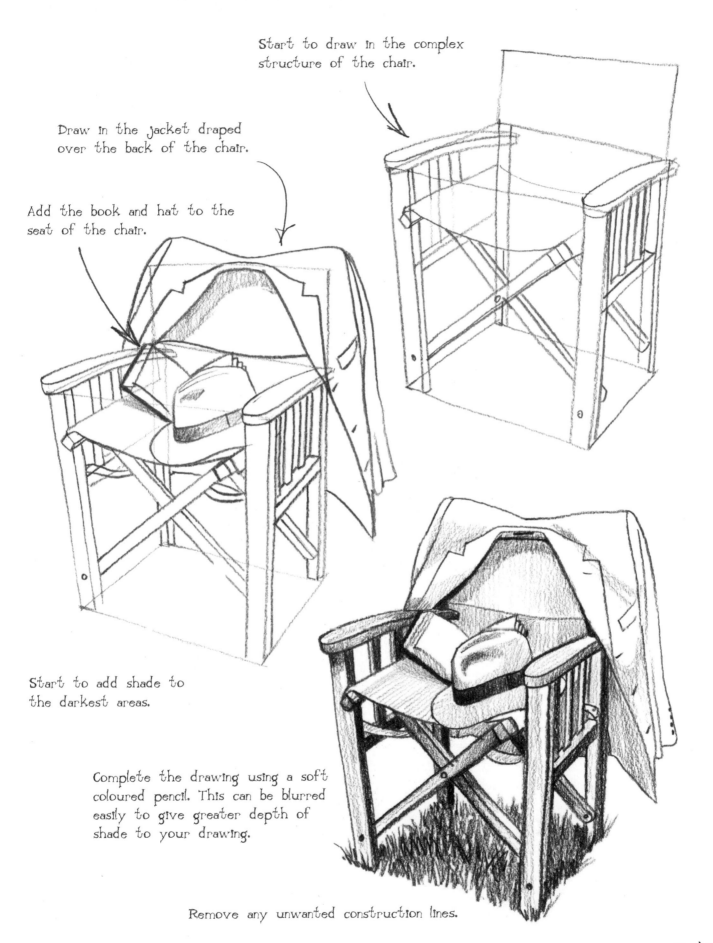

Start to draw in the complex structure of the chair.

Draw in the jacket draped over the back of the chair.

Add the book and hat to the seat of the chair.

Start to add shade to the darkest areas.

Complete the drawing using a soft coloured pencil. This can be blurred easily to give greater depth of shade to your drawing.

Remove any unwanted construction lines.

27

Flotsam and jetsam

This is a perfect example of a found still life consisting of items washed up on a beach.

Some still-life compositions occur naturally. Keep your eyes open for them when you are out and about.

Start by sketching out the positions of the main elements.

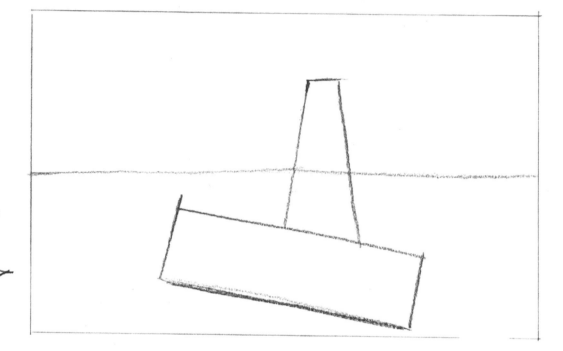

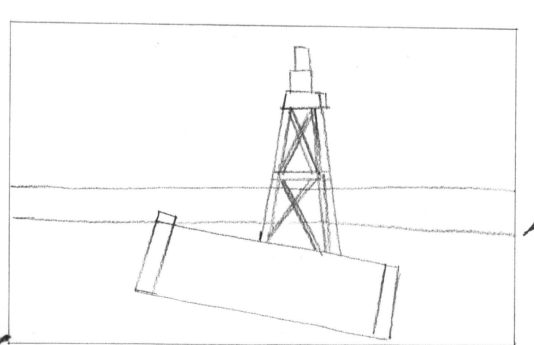

Now add more details and the shoreline behind.

Draw in more of the objects. Start adding detail.

Complete all remaining details. The direction of the light source is often less obvious in outside scenes. Look carefully at your objects to see how light and shade affect and define them.

Remove any unwanted construction lines.

29

Bowl of fruit

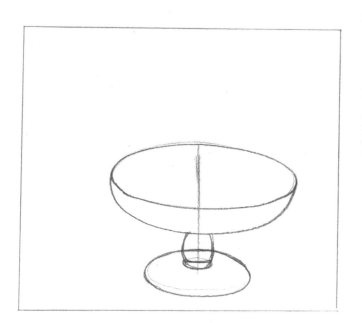

A bowl of fruit is a classic still-life composition. Many famous artists have drawn still lifes of fruit. It is worth researching other artists for inspiration!

Start by sketching out the shape of the bowl as a wire-frame outline.

Sketch in the shape of the overlapping fruit. Keep these construction lines faint so they can be easily erased.

Using a mirror

Try looking at your drawing in a mirror. Seeing it in reverse can help you spot mistakes.

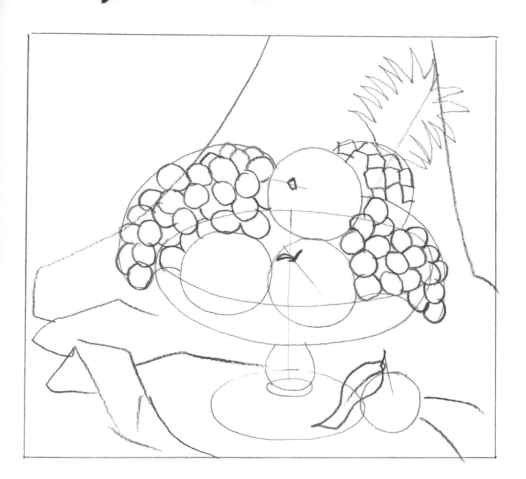

Indicate the folds of the drapery. Add more form and detail to the fruit shapes.

Add shading to the individual fruit and the various parts of the bowl. This will give your finished drawing a three-dimensional effect.

Glossary

Composition The arrangement of the various parts of a picture on the drawing paper.

Construction lines Guidelines used in the early stages of a drawing which are usually erased later.

Cross–hatching A series of criss–crossing lines used to add shade to a drawing.

Ellipse An oval. Circles appear as ellipses when they are seen in perspective.

Found composition A composition in which objects are shown just as the artist found them, rather than being arranged by the artist.

Hatching A series of parallel lines used to add shade to a drawing.

Light source The direction from which the light seems to come in a drawing.

Memento mori A traditional type of still–life picture designed to remind people that life is short.

Silhouette A drawing that shows only a dark shape, like a shadow.

Three–dimensional Having an effect of depth, so as to look lifelike or real.

Vanishing point The place in a perspective drawing where parallel lines appear to meet.

Wire–frame outline A drawing which shows only the outside shape of an object, as if it were a flat shape made of bent wire.

Index